Discovering Brady

Wanda Carolina Santos

illustrated by Antim Marius

www.deveostudio.com

ISBN: 978-1-969463-73-0

This book is dedicated to my loving nephew, Jakobe Rosado, who was a huge inspiration when I decided to become an author. Jakobe, was diagnosed with autism when he was two years old and he has embraced his unique differences his whole life. He has taught our family the value of inclusion, kindness, creativity and acceptance. Jakobe best known as "Kobe" sees past the disability, he sees people.

The goal of this book is to inspire and empower kids and the adults around them about what bullying is and how they can help prevent it from happening to anyone else. Together as one collective community we can foster a better future for all children. Be like Brady and embrace your own unique abilities no matter how different they may be from others. Having self-confidence is the most valuable trait you can possess in life because it allows you to constantly work towards achieving your goals without the fear of failure and self-doubt.

This new children's book series is more than just a story—it's a movement to show the power of resilience, strength, and self-love.

Inspired by my incredible 10-year-old nephew, Jakobe, who was diagnosed with autism at just 2 years old, Discovering Brady was created to shine a light on what truly matters: compassion, confidence, and embracing our differences. Each book will highlight a different challenge a child may face, which will be then followed by an incredibly inspiring storyline that shows their resilience through overcoming these obstacles.

Jakobe has a gift—he sees no disability, no limitations—
just people.
His inspiring spirit guided the creation of Brady, a young
boy who faces bullying because of his disability, but finds
courage within himself to rise above and inspire others to
change.

Together, we can teach children everywhere that
challenges don't define us—our strength and kindness do.

Support Discovering Brady by sharing it with families,
educators, and communities. Let's raise awareness, spark
conversations, and empower kids to embrace who they are
with confidence and pride.

Because every child deserves to see themselves as the
hero of their story.

Once upon a time, in a small friendly town, there lived a little boy named Brandon Sanchez. Brandon, also known as, "Brady," was a kind-hearted and imaginative 9-year-old boy, who had a gleam of curiosity in his eyes everywhere he went. Born in the Dominican Republic as an only child, Brady moved to the United States with his parents at 5 years old. His devoted parents worked tirelessly, saving every penny to give him a better life in America.

Moving was both scary and exciting for Brady. He wished his extended family, and friends could join him but was thrilled at the thought of traveling across the country and having the opportunity to experience real snow for the very first time.

After moving, Brady's family settled in the small town of Methuen, Massachusetts. Soon after, he started attending a new school where he was a model student, however, he was different from his peers. Brady had one thing that made him different from the other children at school; he walked with a slight limp from his right leg that required him to walk with a cane.

You see, Brady was born with a rare disease that causes pressure buildup and inflammation throughout his body, causing his arms and legs to stiffen up on most days. This disease affected his mobility the most. Brady lived in pain every day.

From the moment Brady steps into the schoolyard, he is faced with unpleasant word exchanges and unkind gestures from his classmates. Brady was being bullied and it was happening every single day. They would mimic his limp, call him names, and make fun of him repeatedly. This hurt Brady deeply, as he longed to be accepted just like everybody else.

Brady never considered himself different from his classmates in the Dominican Republic, but here he began to see his disability as a negative distraction and a limitation. The once overly confident young boy was starting to feel insecure about himself and his unique differences. Despite the constant bullying, Brady was sad often, but he never lost hope. He found solace in his vivid imagination, which transported him to magical realms where he was accepted and celebrated for his uniqueness. His imagination gave him strength, reminding him that he was special, and that his limp did not define him.

One day, during recess, Brady stumbled upon an old book in the school library, called "To the Rescue Superheroes". The pages were filled with tales of heroes who overcame great obstacles despite their very own unique differences. Inspired by their stories, Brady decided it was time to change his very own story.

With determination and shining in his eyes, Brady began to practice walking without a limp or his cane. He would spend hours every day, strengthening his leg and honing his balance. Though he stumbled and fell many times, he never gave up. Brady knew that his journey to becoming more confident in himself was not going to be an easy one, but he was ready to face it head-on.

As the days turned into weeks, Brady's classmates noticed a big change in him. He carried himself with newfound confidence, his head held high, his hair slicked back, and a smile playing on his lips. The bullies were taken aback, for they no longer had the power to hurt him. Brady, although still needing to use his cane, he walked with confidence, courage, and conviction. Brady felt like he was on top of the world!

Intrigued by his new and bold transformation, some of the other children approached Brady, curious about his secret. Brady, embracing his newfound self-assurance, shared his story with them. He explained that he had learned to embrace his differences, focusing on his strengths rather than his limitations. To their surprise, the children found themselves captivated by Brady's words. They began to see him not as someone to mock, but as someone to admire. Brady's resilience and unwavering spirit touched their hearts, and they realized they should have never bullied him. They all apologized in that very moment.

From that day forward, Brady's classmates rallied around him. They stood up against bullying, spreading a message of acceptance and inclusivity.

The once divided school became a united community, where everyone was celebrated for their unique abilities. As time went on, Brady's limp became a symbol of strength, and overcoming adversity. He became a role model for others, teaching them to embrace their differences and to never let anyone define their worth.

Brady's story did not end at the schoolyard. Word of his journey spread throughout the town, inspiring not only children but adults as well. Parents, teachers, and community members rallied around Brady, supporting his message of acceptance and kindness. Since then, every year a celebration is held at the school, in Brady's name, celebrating everyone's differences.

Brady is now in high school, and he is on their Anti-Bullying Committee where he works closely with other students and teachers to find ways of reaching out to students who are actively being bullied as well as creating safe spaces for kids to talk about their emotions and mental health needs. Brady plans to go off to college to become a psychologist in hopes of helping more children and their families towards self-acceptance, mental health and general wellbeing.

THE END

Wanda Santos

About the Author

Wanda Santos is the Vice President of Community Living at Waystone Health & Human Services, where she has dedicated nearly two decades to serving individuals with disabilities across the Merrimack Valley. With a career in human services that began at just 16 years old, Wanda has become a trusted leader, mentor, and advocate for families and caregivers.

In addition to her professional role, Wanda is a certified Integrative Trauma Coach and Practitioner, specializing in somatic healing, mindfulness, and breathwork. She is the founder of Roses of Renewal, a growing community movement that creates safe, healing spaces through workshops, events, and conversations centered on resilience, wellness, and connection.

As an author and storyteller, Wanda uses her voice to bring awareness to issues that deeply matter—disability inclusion, mental health advocacy, caregiver burnout, and family resilience. Her upcoming works include children's books inspired by her nephews' journey with their own disabilities and the strength it requires daily.

A proud Latina and community organizer, Wanda is committed to bringing compassionate leadership, equity, and fresh perspectives to her community. She believes in creating spaces where every voice matters and where kindness and resilience drive change.

When she's not working or organizing, Wanda nurtures her love for travel, meditation, journaling and cultural connection, always seeking new ways to balance service to others with self-care.

For more information, contact: InspiredbyWanda@gmail.com

💚 You Are Never Alone
Just like Brady, you have a special light inside you —
one that shines even when things feel hard.
If someone ever makes you feel sad or left out,
remember: there are people who care deeply about
you and want to help.

You can always:

- Talk to a trusted grown-up — like a parent, teacher, or school counselor.
- Call or text 988 if you ever feel scared, worried, or need someone kind to listen.
- Visit StompOutBullying.org for ideas on staying safe and standing up for kindness.

Your voice matters.
Your feelings matter.
And there will always be helping hands ready to lift you up.